ESSENTIAL BASS GUITAR TECHNIQUES

21 Skills Every Serious Player Should Master

by Chris Kringel

To access audio visit:
www.halleonard.com/mylibrary

Enter Code
2918-5432-6556-7737

ISBN 978-1-4803-4240-8

HAL•LEONARD®
CORPORATION

7777 W. BLUEMOUND RD. P.O. BOX 13819 MILWAUKEE, WI 53213

In Australia Contact:
Hal Leonard Australia Pty. Ltd.
4 Lentara Court
Cheltenham, Victoria, 3192 Australia
Email: ausadmin@halleonard.com.au

TABLE OF CONTENTS

Page

INTRODUCTION

Welcome to *Essential Bass Guitar Techniques*. The focus of this book is on the physical technique of playing the bass guitar. I will introduce you to a variety of ways to technically approach the bass guitar so that you will be able to execute or perform with confidence in any musical situation.

Refining your bass skills will allow you to creatively express your musical vision in an artistic fashion. Technique will be your vehicle to accomplish any activity or task as it relates to the bass. To put it simply: the more technique you have under your belt, the more options you have with which to express yourself. Take away the limitations of technique, and you can perform anything you want with relative ease. Just as a painter is only limited by his or her imagination and technical ability, the same can be said for any form of art or activity. First, one must have the will to create. Then, one must have some form of technical ability in order to execute their creation.

This book is a reference guide, so reading it front to back is unnecessary. It's set up so that you can pick and choose what you'd like to work on. Feel free to jump to any technique or area of interest. However, even if you are familiar with certain techniques, it never hurts to remain open to another perspective on execution. One of the most compelling things about music is that it's a lifelong journey; there is always room for expansion and improvement.

The techniques in this book are laid out with reference to your plucking (or picking) hand, your fingering hand, and, in some cases, by technique alone. If you are right-handed, the plucking hand is usually the right hand, and the fingering hand is usually the left. This book is a guide and is by no means "the law". Take the concepts, build off of them, improve on them, and, if you find a better way that fits your physical make up, do that.

Included in this book are various techniques that I feel are essential to any player. They cover most of the situations that will arise when playing the bass guitar. I hope you enjoy this book, and please take your time and be patient with yourself. Learning is not about the finished product; it's about the process and joy of the present experience. If you are new to playing bass, you will soon discover its endless complexity. So have fun! Remember: Curiosity is your best friend when wanting to improve and expand.

Chris Kringel, 2013

MENTAL ATTITUDE

One of the most important—if not the most important—aspects of music and life is your mental attitude. You think thoughts, emotions follow, and then actions arise. In other words, how you think about yourself and the world around you generates your feelings, and your feelings are the fuel that drives you into action. I've found that the mindset of curiosity is helpful and essential to learning. The more curious you are, the more fascinated and eager you will be to explore and learn new things. When you think you know or hide what you don't know, you stop being a student. This can become a hindrance to further development. The best mental approach is to hold both teacher-like qualities of being confident and informative as well as student-like qualities of curiosity and exploration.

THE RECORDING

The audio track icon indicates an example has a corresponding audio track.

Many examples start with a general technique exercise followed by a bass line using the specific technique covered in each area. Bass lines are the tracks with chord changes and are repeated without bass for you to play along.

All tracks are recorded at standard 440 tuning.

All examples performed by Chris Kringel.

Recorded, mixed, and mastered at Santa's Workshop in Pewaukee, WI.

ABOUT THE AUTHOR

Chris Kringel has authored five instructional books and an instructional DVD for Hal Leonard, including *Fretless Bass*, *Funk Bass*, *The Bassist's Guide to Creativity*, and *Play Bass Today* (Volumes 1 and 2). He is also the producer for over 50 Hal Leonard titles, including *Ukulele Play-Along*, *Harmonica Play-Along*, and *Easy Rhythm Guitar*, to name a few. Chris has worked freelance for Hal Leonard as an author, transcriber, editor, proofreader, and producer for over 20 years and has performed internationally as a bassist, band director, sound engineer, and producer for various artists, including Cynic, Portal, Aeon Spoke, Jack Grassel, Fibonacci Sequence, Jason Weber, and Inda Eaton. If you are interested in more information, check out *www.chriskringel.com*.

PLUCKING TECHNIQUES

Finger Style

To play with your fingers, first find a place to rest your thumb. You'll use your fingers to pluck the strings with an upward motion. There are many factors that go into plucking the strings: how you rest your thumb, what fingers you are using, the angle of your hand, and where you place your forearm. There are several nuances that make a difference in the way one can pluck the strings. There are as many ways to play as there are players, so spend some time trying different methods to find out what feels and works best for you. Watch other players—especially your influences—and see how they execute their plucking. A word of caution: Don't bend your wrist too much, especially when resting your forearm on the bass, as this can lead to hand injury! Below are some pictorial examples to visually guide you on how the plucking hand can be positioned on the bass.

Thumb Forward,
Forearm Resting

Thumb in Line,
Forearm Resting

Resting on Angle

Thumb Forward,
Forearm Up

Thumb in Line,
Forearm Up

CAUTION: Bending Wrist

Anchor

One of the first things to consider when plucking is the anchoring of your thumb. Do you keep your thumb anchored on one of the pickups or thumb rest, or does your thumb move to different anchor points (lower strings) when you pluck on the higher strings? There is no one correct way, and my suggestion is to commit to a way and stick to it. Be consistent. When anchoring your thumb on the pickup, you have less movement, but string muting will then come mainly from your fretting hand. If your thumb floats and anchors on lower strings as you play higher strings, the open strings are muted with your thumb as it moves to anchor on the lower strings. This takes more thought and time to execute initially but may pay off with time spent mastering the technique.

Thumb Pickup
Low Strings

Thumb Pickup
High Strings

Thumb Float
Low Strings

Thumb Float
High Strings

The position in which you place your plucking hand in regard to the bridge or the edge of the fingerboard drastically changes your tone. The closer you pluck towards the fingerboard, the deeper and bigger the tone. The closer to the bridge, the brighter and more pronounced the sound. Keep this in mind when finding an anchor point, especially if you anchor on a pickup. Note that the back pickup and front pickup sound different (if you have two pickups), and you can also anchor on the edge of the fretboard. If you anchor on the lower strings, you can float wherever best suits you.

Two or Three Fingers

However many fingers you decide to pluck with depends on your comfort and ability to execute. It's really up to you. The majority of players use two fingers: the index and middle. Some players use three. I've seen very few use four fingers, due to the pinky being much shorter in length. The goal is getting the fingers to work together smoothly and evenly.

When plucking the strings, you can pluck in two different ways:

- **Pluck up (towards your chest or the top of the bass):** This is most common and technically sound.

- **Pluck down (into the bass, toward the body):** This makes the strings bounce against the frets and is used to achieve a heavier sound, though it sacrifices speed and cleanliness.

Here is an example so you can hear the different types of plucking.

Example 1

Follow-Through

The key to a great sound and flawless execution is to have as little movement as possible. Whether you pluck with two or three fingers, the question is this: how much do you move your fingers when plucking? One common technique that really helps speed and clarity is *follow-through*. What you are looking for is a precise flat pluck towards your chest, and after each pluck, the finger rests or follows through to land on the next lower string. To work on follow-through, try plucking the A string with the first finger and have it follow through to the E string below. In other words, the E string will stop your finger. Do the same with your second finger, and you'll notice that your fingers only move as far as the spacing between strings. Minimal movement and good control with the plucking hand will help create a nice, thick, clean tone.

Pluck A String

Rest on E String

Alternating Fingers

For speed and execution, make sure you *alternate* plucking fingers. If you're using a two-finger technique, make sure you alternate between first and second finger with every pluck. If you're using three fingers, make sure you alternate all three.

You will want as little movement as possible when plucking, and as soon as you pluck with the first finger, place your second finger on the string you just plucked to stop it from ringing. As you alternate your fingers, you'll notice with every pluck that your second finger is ready to play as soon as you've plucked the note. It should sound like this:

Example 2

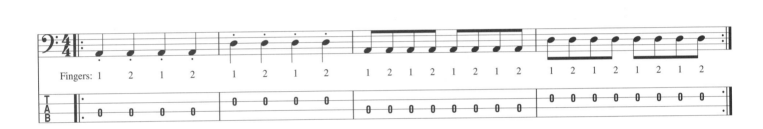

Now let's use the same alternating concept with the three-finger technique. You can approach three-finger plucking in two different ways.

1. Plucking index, middle, and ring finger like alternating with two.

2. Use the index and middle fingers on the lower strings and the middle and ring on the higher strings. The middle finger will be going back and forth, while the index stays on the lower strings and the ring stays on the higher strings. Remember to pluck with the index finger and then immediately put the middle finger in place to play. Pluck with the middle and then place the index on the string to mute it. The ring finger was already resting on the higher string, ready to pluck, and the middle is moving to play the higher string immediately after the ring is finished plucking. One advantage of this method is that you can string skip and mute all strings with the plucking hand. To accentuate the muting, all the notes should be short.

Index and Middle Fingers on the Lower Strings

Middle and Ring Fingers on the Higher Strings

Example 3

Fingers: 1   2   3   2   1   2   3   2   1   2   3   2   1   2   3   2

The tendency for most players is to brush quickly over the plucking hand and move on. I suggest making time to develop your plucking hand by going slowly in order to build muscle memory. Spend some time every practice session on plucking technique. Just like tying your shoe, at first, it takes concentration because you've never done it before. Over time, it becomes so natural that you don't have to think about it. Remember to have fun and, with all the examples in the book, take them and mix up the rhythm, change the notes, etc. Be creative and make permutations of each one to keep practice fresh and new. A big part of music is the creative aspect, so keep that part alive and well by exploring different ways to expand on the exercises given.

Here's an exercise using groups of two, three, and four at three different tempos with each repeat. If you're plucking with two fingers, simply alternate index and middle. If you're plucking with three fingers, try both ways: First alternate index, middle, and ring. Next, try index and middle on the E and A strings and the middle and ring on the D and G strings. In the example below, the speed increases with each repeat, but it does not have to be played that way. Pick a tempo that is comfortable for you.

Example 4

Economy of Motion

You will notice that when playing finger style, that sometimes your finger is already resting on the string you have to pluck next. In this case, alternating doesn't make much sense. This is what I call *economy of motion*. For example: you pluck the A string with your index finger, and your index finger follows through to rest on the E string. If the next note you need to play is on the E string, pluck with the index finger, as opposed to alternating and using the middle finger. Using natural movement versus implementing strict rules can save motion and help facilitate a natural and smooth technique.

The next few exercises are all about your plucking hand. Your fretting hand will just mute the strings to create a dead or muted sound for the first half of the example. I will also give you some options on finger order while plucking.

You'll notice some different choices in the plucking of this next exercise due to following through and economy of motion. The finger is already on the string because I followed through from the previous pluck. You will notice this happening especially when you go from high to low. Take this one slowly and really pay attention to how this concept maximizes movement. I have a two-finger and three-finger option for you to reference.

Example 5

For this one, we will pluck triplets. When working with three fingers, some combination of finger plucks will be up to each individual. Try what I have suggested, and then try some other combinations. For this exercise, when going from high to low, you can use the ring finger to follow behind and mute the higher strings.

Example 6

Here's another short exercise based on a groove in G. Try this not only with economy of motion, but also with alternating to see what works best for you. Again, there is no "right" way to do this. What's important is that you try several different ways. There are example fingerings between the notation and tab staves for you to try. Remember to go slowly and see what feels best. At first, you may choose to keep things simple and consistent by alternating, but in time, you may find economy of motion to be more fluid. Over time, muscle memory takes over, and you won't have to pay as much attention to every finger pluck. On the audio, this next exercise will repeat without bass so you can play along.

Example 7

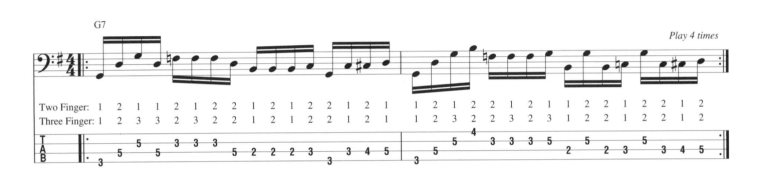

Dynamics

Another way to really master plucking-hand technique is to practice dynamics. In musical terms, dynamics indicates the loudness of music. On a technical level, dynamics are about controlling the amount of attack with each pluck of the string. Using dynamics helps with technique development and control. It also creates feel or groove by accenting certain beats within each measure. For the next few exercises, we'll use the accent mark (>) to indicate when you should strike the string with more force. To keep this simple, we'll use only soft and accented (slightly louder) as the two dynamic variations.

This is a standard blues bass line that's fun to play and will help develop technique. You'll be string skipping and controlling your string attack. It will also be obvious that the accents help the groove, since you'll be accenting on beats 2 and 4 along with the snare drum. On the audio, this one repeats without bass.

Example 8

This one is more of a technique exercise, so really concentrate on the dynamic control and see how you do.

Example 9

You can take the concept of dynamics as far as you want. I suggest that you push yourself and explore, because working with dynamics significantly develops muscle memory. It's very subtle but highly effective. You can also expand the range of dynamics from soft (piano, *p*) to medium soft (mezzo-piano, *mp*) to medium loud (mezzo-forte, *mf*) to loud (forte, *f*). Of course, if you study music, you know that you have far more options than these four, as well. The idea here is about finger control and mastering the use of your plucking hand. The more hand control that you have, the more ability you will posses to express yourself without technical limitations.

Thumb

Using your thumb to pluck the strings is another way to get the job done. It consists of downstrokes and is pretty simple to do. Rest your fingers on the higher strings and pluck with your thumb. Go to any of the previous examples and play them with your thumb instead of fingers, and try this next example as well. After the repeats, the audio will play without bass so you can play along.

Example 10

Palm Muting

Palm muting is basically self-explanatory—you rest your palm lightly on the strings to slightly mute them while plucking. The closer to the bridge you place your palm, the more the notes will ring out. The farther you are from the bridge, the more the notes will be muted. This is a great technique for various styles and helps add a different texture to your bass lines.

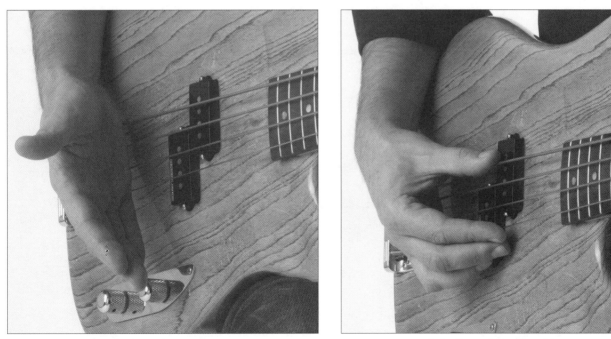

Palm Rested, On Strings   Palm Rested, Ready to Play

When palm muting, you can pluck with your thumb, fingers, or use a combination. For the next two examples, try plucking with your thumb only, then try with your index and middle, and, lastly, with your thumb, index, and middle. Place your palm close to the bridge and then move it forward an inch and notice the change in tone. The rationale behind these examples (and book) is to explore various options. See what works for you in regard to what feels physically comfortable as well as what sounds good to you. The examples repeat for you to play along with.

Example 11

Example 12

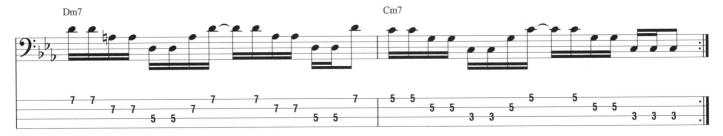

PICKING TECHNIQUES

Standard Picking

To play with a pick, grip it between the thumb and index or thumb and middle finger. Keep the rest of your hand relaxed and strike the strings in a downward motion. The fingers not holding the pick may curve under or rest on the bass. As you might imagine, there are many nuances to holding a pick: how it rests against your finger, where you hold the pick, and whether you use more of a wrist-like motion or your forearm to pluck. You can even use a thumb pick, but the same theory applies. Watch multiple players, especially your influences, and see how they execute using a pick. Find what is most comfortable for you. The next step is putting the time in until it feels natural and flowing. Any technique may feel unnatural at first, but over time, practice creates patterns of muscle memory, and those patterns are going to be the foundation for your technique. Make sure you take your time and create patterns that don't create problems for you.

Thumb/Index

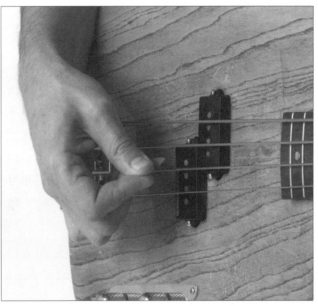
Thumb/Middle

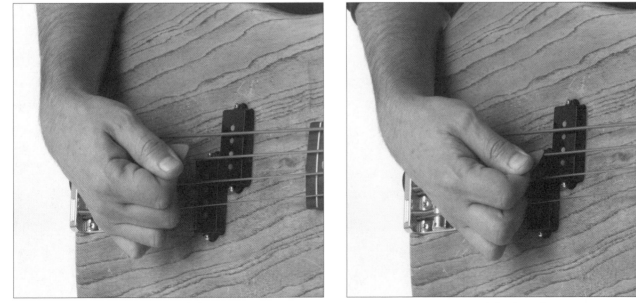
Hand Curled

Hand Anchored

To get you started, let's practice a simple bass line picking exercise, using all downstrokes.

Example 13

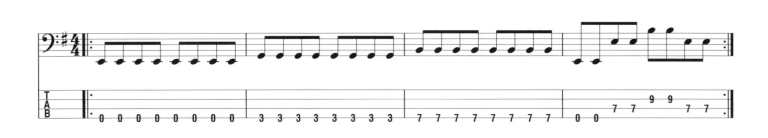

Palm Muting with a Pick

This is just like palm muting in the previous section. Rest your palm lightly on the strings to slightly mute them while using a pick to pluck the strings. The farther in from the bridge you move your palm, the more the notes will be muted.

To clean up any unnecessary string ring, use palm muting to mute the strings abruptly or slowly after playing a part. In other words, play the part, and then follow by quickly using your palm to mute the strings. Apply a fast or slow mute, depending on where you place your palm and how much pressure you use. Experiment with the example below. The example will mute quickly at first, and mute less as the example develops.

Example 14

In this example, the bass line is palm muted the first two times it is played, and the last two times, it is palm muted for only half the time. Palm muting is a great way to change the dynamics and timbre of a part.

Example 15

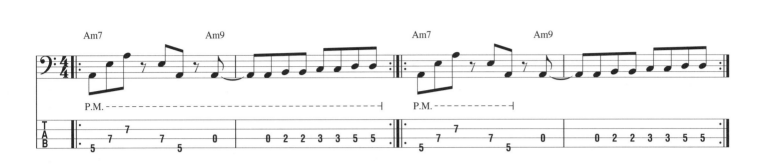

The best way to get good at anything is to practice. If you like the sound palm muting creates, make time and have fun experimenting with it.

Alternate Picking

You might have noticed that you can use both upstrokes and downstrokes when using a pick. *Alternate picking* is the technique of using a downstroke followed by an upstroke. This pattern is the basis for many players' picking-hand technique. It enables far less movement, which results in quicker execution. Choosing to alternate can depend on tempo or what kind of sound you are going after. It can be awkward to alternate when playing at a slow tempo, and some bass parts sound heavier when played with all downstrokes. Try it out and see how it works for you.

The next exercise will use downstrokes when playing eighth notes and change to alternate picking for the 16th notes.

Example 16

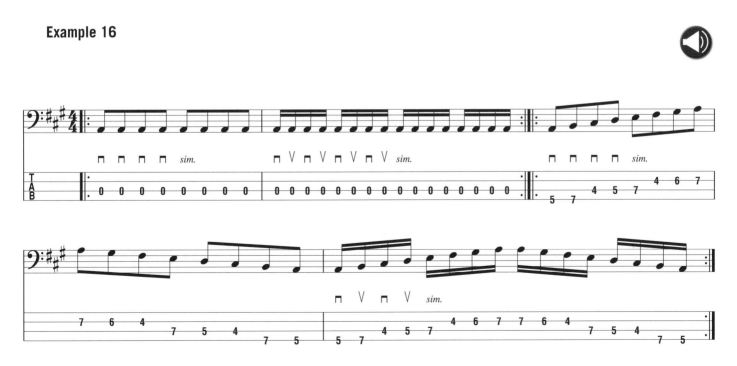

Concentrate on synchronizing your picking hand with your fretting hand. Being able to put your two hands together is critical when playing fast passages with a lot of harmonic movement. This example increases tempo with each repeat.

Example 17

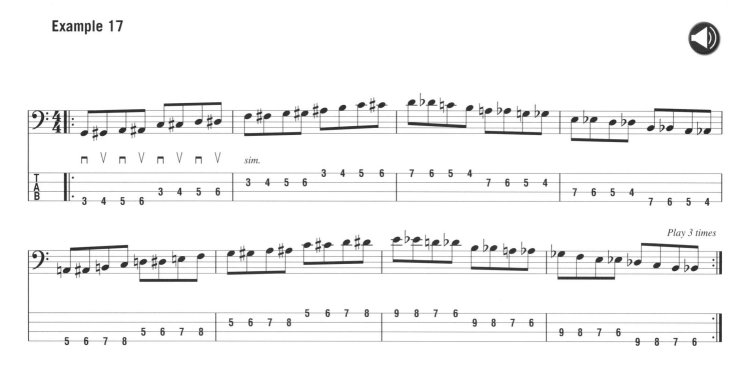

As you can see, Example 17 is a pattern-based exercise using a 1–2–3–4/4–3–2–1 finger pattern that moves up in half steps. If you'd like to extend the exercise by continuing up the neck, please do. You can also change the pattern to 4–3–2–1/1–2–3–4 or 1–3–2–4/4–2–3–1, etc. As you might expect, if you take some time to explore different fingering patterns on this one, you can come up with multiple combinations of your own. I encourage you to do so.

Let's double up on the notes for a shorter exercise. Again, this will increase in tempo with each repeat.

Example 18

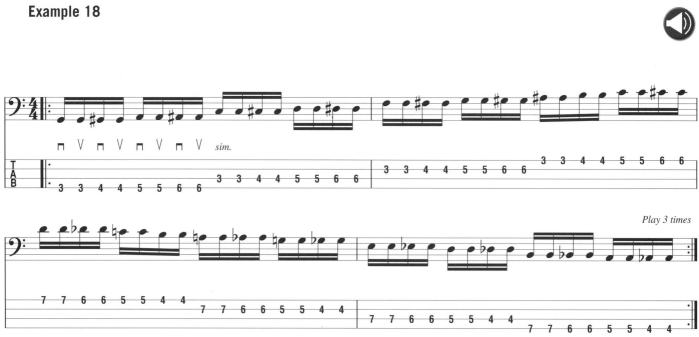

This exercise uses some two-string cross play. This is a G major scale in 3rds. Speed will increase with each repeat.

Example 19

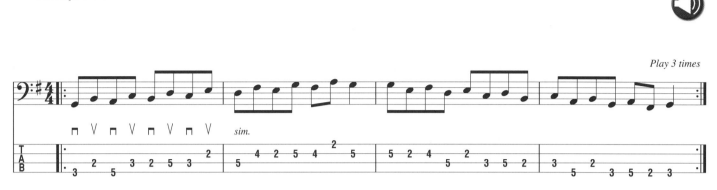

The whole idea of alternate picking is to alternate between downstrokes and upstrokes when playing steady 16th notes (or very fast eighth notes), no matter what you do. Keep it consistent.

Economy Picking

Economy picking is a form of alternate picking with a different twist. The difference is, when crossing to another string, you continue the same picking direction whenever possible. For example, if you're picking on the E string with a dowstroke, upstroke, and downstroke, then when moving to the A string, your pick is naturally ready for a downstroke. You will notice when crossing strings that alternating isn't always the best choice if following the motion of your picking stroke is taken into account. A main point to remember with economy picking is to move your pick across two strings with one continuous motion. Most people use a combination of wrist and forearm to execute economy picking: wrist for alternate picking on one string, and forearm when dragging or crossing to the upper or lower string. Let's go to an example so we can put the theory into action.

Example 20

Here are two different licks to demonstrate the technique.

Example 21

A great way to practice economy picking is to practice scales and other patterns with plenty of movement between strings.

Example 22

FRET-HAND TECHNIQUES

Position

Let's take a look at positioning the fret hand. For most readers, the fret hand will be the left hand, and for lefties, it will be the right hand. Keep your fingers curved at each joint but relaxed. Use your fingertips to fret the notes. The thumb should touch the back of the neck to keep position, but be careful not to grip the neck or to press hard and create too much tension. The index and pinky fingers should line up horizontally on the neck, and the thumb should line up with them on the back of the neck. Vertically, the thumb is somewhere between the index and pinky; it will float up and down along with the movement of the fingers, depending on what strings you play. If you plant the thumb, you will find that your wrist is bending in some uncomfortable ways, so remember that the thumb floats along with the fingers, and the wrist stays slightly bent.

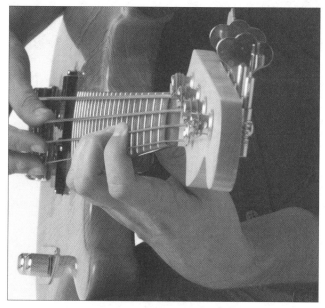

Hand

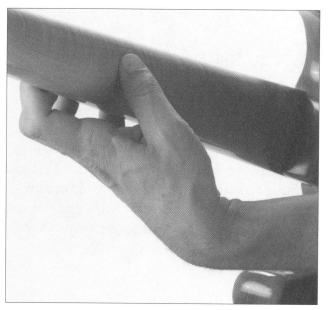

Wrist

Front Neck

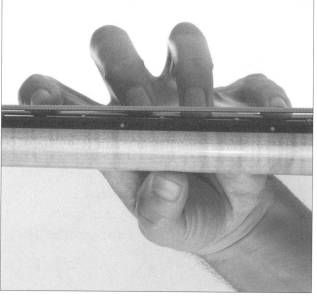

Top Neck

When fretting a note, place your fingers close to the fret wire; the clearest tone usually comes from being as close to the fret as possible.

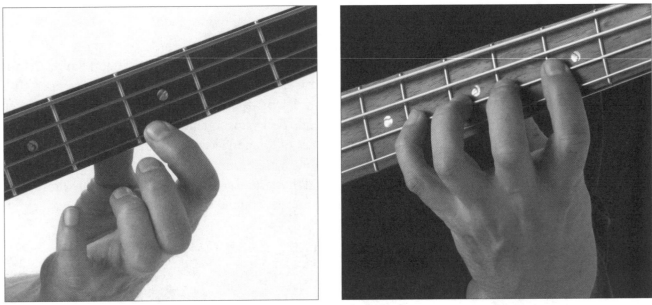

| Fret Close Up | Fret Hand |

For all the exercises, keep your fingers as close to the strings as possible. Some players get into a habit of lifting their fingers up because they simply haven't thought about keeping them down. Lifting your fingers up can create extra noise and slow you down technically. Keeping your fret-hand fingers close to the strings will take extra effort and time at first, but in the end, you will be rewarded. Remember: practice makes patterns—not perfection. If you practice bad habits, you will end up having to correct them in the future, and that can take even more time.

Finger Dexterity

Let's work on some exercises to get you started with your fret hand. For explanation purposes, we'll number the fingers as follows:

1 = Index

2 = Middle

3 = Ring

4 = Pinky

This one starts on the seventh fret because it is technically easier for hand position—especially when starting. Keep each finger down after it is played; by the time you play the fourth finger, and all four fingers should be on the string. Go slowly at first, taking time to fret each note and get a good, solid tone, and then gradually speed up. The example will increase in speed with each repeat.

Example 23

Here's an exercise much like the previous one. Keep your fingers as close to the strings without touching after each note is played. Notice that you can keep finger 2 down when playing 4, and 1 down when playing 3. Remember to play close to the fret. This example will increase in speed with each repeat, but the main point is tone and execution—not speed.

Example 24

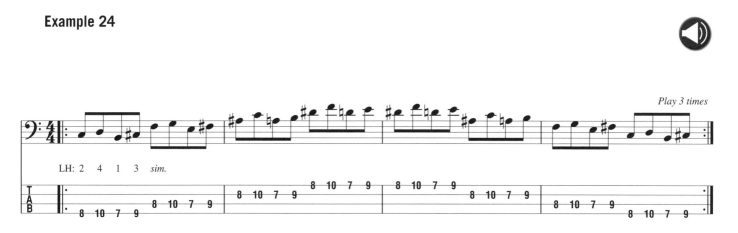

All of these patterns focus on finger sequence and can be moved to different locations on the neck. They are great technique exercises to build finger dexterity and independence. Here are some permutations to work with when playing any four-finger exercises:

1–2–3–4, 1–2–4–3, 1–3–2–4, 1–3–4–2, 1–4–2–3, 1–4–3–2

2–1–3–4, 2–1–4–3, 2–3–1–4, 2–3–4–1, 2–4–1–3, 2–4–3–1

3–1–2–4, 3–1–4–2, 3–2–1–4, 3–2–4–1, 3–4–1–2, 3–4–2–1

4–1–2–3, 4–1–3–2, 4–2–1–3, 4–2–3–1, 4–3–1–2, 4–3–2–1

This is a three-finger sequence that leaves out the first finger, which is great to do when you want to build strength in the other three fingers.

Example 25

Here are some three-finger patterns that omit the first finger:

2–3–4, 2–4–3, 3–2–4, 3–4–2, 4–2–3, 4–3–2

This exercise works on form while moving across the strings. Keep each finger down as you play the next note. Do this ascending (1–2–3–4), shift fingers, and then descend (1–2–3–4). You can move this same pattern anywhere on the neck.

Example 26

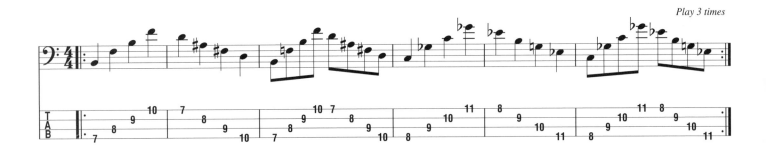

This next exercise is helpful for bending and building up strength in each finger. Keep each finger planted after it is played—do not lift it. Play four notes (four fingers down) and start again. Go slowly and don't worry about timing. If it's painful, stop and build up to the full stretch.

Example 27

Barre

Playing each note with your finger tips or moving your fingers to another string isn't always convenient. Sometimes, you have to fret a note with another part of your finger, especially when it's vertically available under the currently fretted note. This is called *barring*. It requires you to straighten out your finger and play each note between the joints of the flattened finger.

Barre First Finger

Barre Third Finger

Here is an exercise that works on barring two strings. It speeds up on each repeat.

Example 28

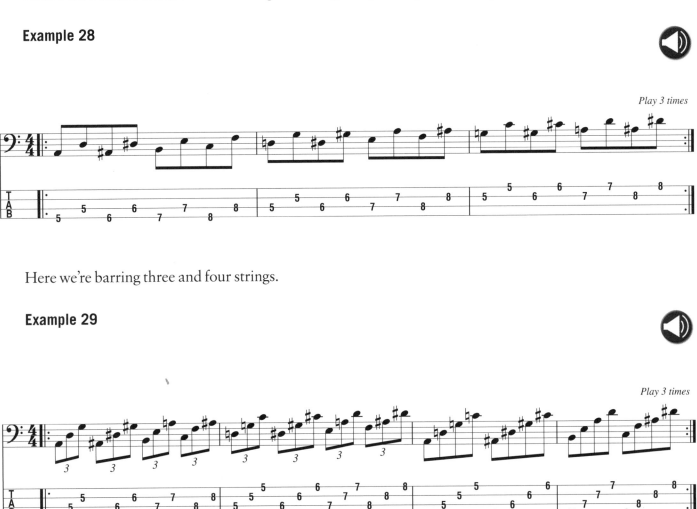

Here we're barring three and four strings.

Example 29

Fret-Hand Muting

Fret-hand muting is another topic that usually goes unmentioned, yet it's essential to maintaining a clean, precise tone—especially when playing tight staccato bass lines. Fret-hand muting consists of lightly touching with your fretting hand any open strings that are ringing—basically stopping the string in motion. If you're playing a fretted note, simply lift your finger up slightly to stop the string from ringing. When combined with plucking-hand muting, one can eliminate any unwanted string ring while playing any bass part. For the next exercise, mute the open strings by lightly touching them and/or lifting up and mute any fretted notes whenever you see a rest.

Example 30

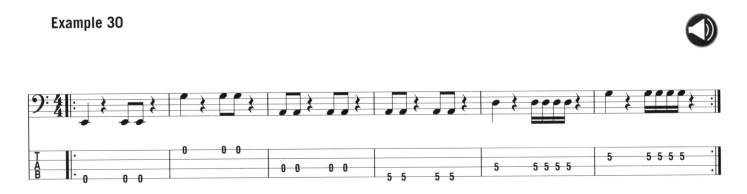

Dead Notes

Dead notes refer to the act of muting the string while plucking to make a percussive sound without any actual pitch. They help "move air" and add rhythm to your bass lines. Just like muting, all you do is lightly touch the string with your fret hand and then pluck. Be careful not to touch lightly over the fret wire, because that will often create a harmonic, and what we're looking for is a dead/percussive sound.

For this next exercise, we will add dead notes on the same string that you are already playing. Once again, the exercises will repeat without bass.

Example 31

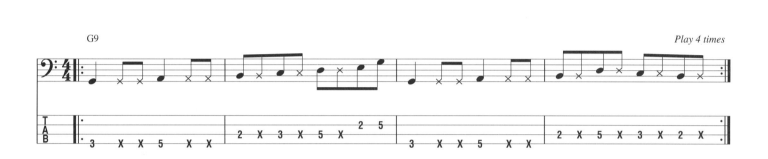

This one is a little trickier. We will be using dead notes on the lower string to create a deep, thick, percussive sound.

Example 32

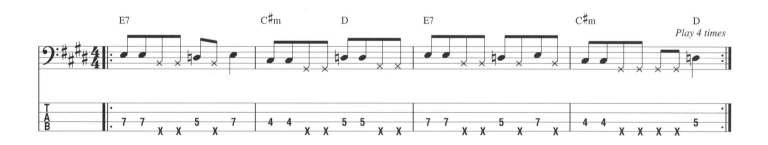

On this one, we will be using dead notes on the higher string to create a brighter percussive tone.

Example 33

Staccato

The duration or length of each note has a huge effect on the groove and sound of your bass line. *Staccato* means playing notes in a short, clipped manner, which creates a tight, punchy sound. When fretting a note, lift up slightly to shorten the note while still touching the string. Instead of writing out rests in notation between notes, we can use a dot over or under each note to indicate staccato. Notice how much the feel changes by adding staccato notes.

Example 34

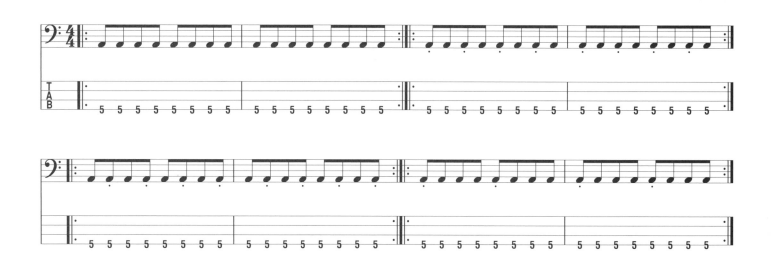

Legato

Legato means to play each note for its full duration. For stringed instruments, it also implies that two or more notes are connected, although only the first note is picked or plucked. This produces a smooth, flowing, connected sound and involves several other techniques, including hammer-ons, pull-offs, and slides.

Here's a legato bass line in which each note rings fully. This kind of bass part can fill a great amount of sonic space.

Example 35

Hammer-ons

To play a *hammer-on*, place one of your fingers on a fret and pluck that note. While the note is ringing, "hammer" another finger onto a higher-pitched note on the same string. Make the motion quickly and forcefully and remember to maintain pressure on the string with the hammered finger.

Hammer-on (Lift)

Hammer-on (Down)

Play a G note at the fifth fret of the D string with your first finger, then hammer on an A note with your third finger at the seventh fret of the same string. Try to achieve the same volume with plucked and hammered notes. Practice this exercise all over the neck, in different locations and on different strings.

Example 36

Hammer-ons can also slur several notes together. Remember to pick or pluck only the first note in each group.

Example 37

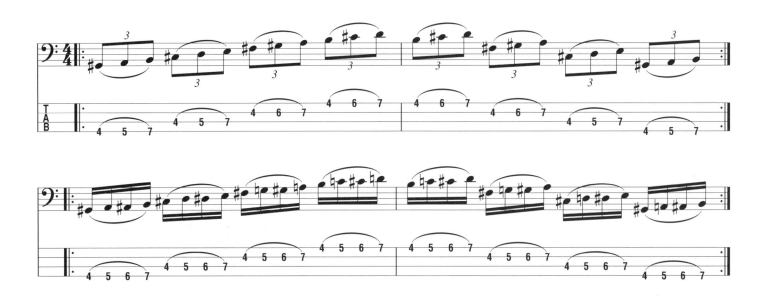

Here's a typical bass line using hammer-ons.

Example 38

Pull-offs

A *pull-off* can be thought of as the opposite of a hammer-on, but really only because one ascends in pitch, while the other descends. The technique is actually considerably different. First, fret *two notes* at once on the same string. Pick or pluck the higher note and then pull off the string in a downward motion, causing the lower note to sound. You're essentially plucking the string with the pull-off finger.

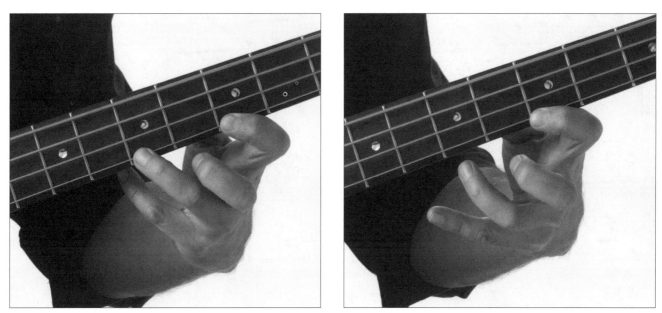

Pull-off (Down)   Pull-off (Pulled)

For this next example, place your third finger on the D note at the seventh fret on the G string and, at the same time, place your first finger on the C note at the fifth fret. Pluck the D note, and then pull off the third finger in a downward motion to sound the C. Strive for the same volume with both notes.

Example 39

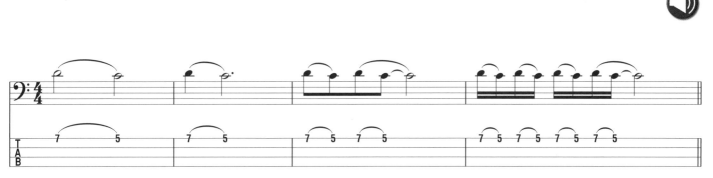

Now let's incorporate three- and four-finger pull-offs. Go slowly and really work on getting it smooth.

Example 40

Take these patterns and create new ones. In other words, experiment! Practice pull-offs in different locations and with different finger combinations and see what you come up with.

Now it's time for a bass line using puff-offs. Again, it will repeat without bass.

Example 41

Trills

Trills are a combination of rapid hammer-ons and pull-offs played together. Usually, the lower note is picked once and then the higher note is sounded in rapid succession by a hammer-on, pull-off, hammer-on, pull-off, and so on. Trills can be technically difficult and also a physical workout on the fingers and forearm, so be careful and rest your hand if pain arises.

Example 42

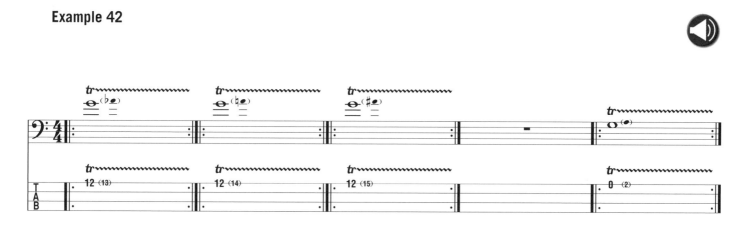

Here's a bass line using a short trill. It will repeat without bass so you can play along, and feel free to create your own bass part after playing the written part.

Example 43

Slides

The *slide* technique is much like the basic concept of a physical slide. One starts at a location and slides while keeping contact with the surface from point A to point B. When playing a slide on a bass, strike a note and slide your finger up or down the neck without releasing pressure on your fretting finger. Sliding is a great technique for adding character and vibe to any bass line.

Here's an example with slides ascending and descending. Some slides are played in time, while others are performed as a grace note, which is more like a nuance or ornament before a note. Technically speaking, the time value is so quick for a grace note that it is written in notation as a mini-note with a slash through it.

Example 44

Here is a bass line using slides.

Example 45

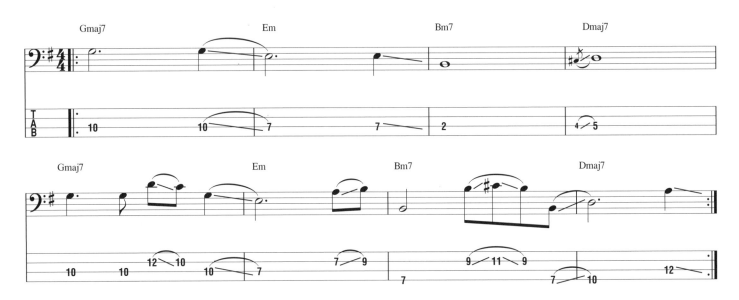

Vibrato

Another technique to add a little more expression to your bass playing is *vibrato*. Vibrato can range from very subtle to very noticeable, depending on your taste and how it's used. There are three basic ways to achieve vibrato:

- **Bend vibrato:** This is done by pushing and pulling the string up and down (toward the ceiling and toward the floor), using your wrist in a rotating motion, back and forth, or by using your forearm. In this type of vibrato, the pitch will fluctuate between slightly sharp and in tune.

- **Pivot vibrato:** This is achieved by pivoting your fretting finger right to left (toward the nut and then toward the bridge). This vibrato style works best on a fretless bass. On a fretted bass, the effect is much more subtle. The pitch will fluctuate between slightly flat and slightly sharp, producing an average "in tune" pitch.

- **Shake:** A shake is a mix between a slide and pivot vibrato. Instead of pivoting your finger slightly back and forth, you rapidly slide over the fret back and forth.

For this example, I will play each vibrato twice: first subtly, and then more pronounced.

Example 46

For this example, we will work with vibrato. Whether you use bend vibrato or pivot vibrato is up to you; it's really about what feels more natural.

Example 47

Here is a slow, simple, melodic bass part using vibrato.

Example 48

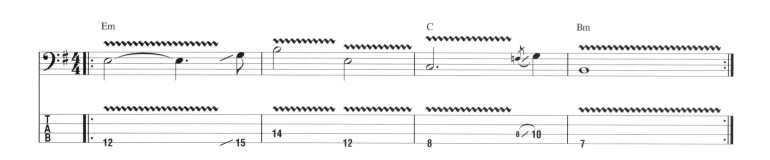

Bending

String bending allows us to emulate the scooped notes of the human voice. It also enables us to hit some "in between" notes. Bending a string raises its pitch; the farther you bend, the higher the pitch. Due to the bigger strings on a bass guitar, bending isn't a staple technique (as it is on lead guitar), though it is used on occasion. It's basically the same technique as bend vibrato but with the intention of bending to (and sometimes releasing from) a specific note.

Here is a bass line example incorporating the bend technique.

Example 49

HARMONICS

Harmonics are overtones located at specific points, or "nodes," on the string. They add a wonderful timbre that goes above and beyond the instrument's normal tone. Mechanically, they are fun an interesting to play. Let's look at the two main types of harmonics associated with the bass guitar: natural and artificial harmonics.

Natural Harmonics

Natural harmonics are the most widely used and normally the first type learned on the bass. They're produced by lightly touching the string (don't push down to the fretboard) with your fret hand at specific points (nodes). You then pluck or pick the string and quickly remove your fret hand while the harmonic rings out. Touching different locations along the string produces different pitches. If you're interested in the science of harmonics and overtones, check out the *harmonic series* in a brief online search or in a more in-depth book.

The easiest harmonic to create is at the 12th fret, which is exactly halfway between the nut and the bridge. Touch the E string lightly *directly over the 12th fret wire* (not in between the frets, as in standard fretting), pluck the string, and then remove your fret hand immediately. You should hear an E note an octave higher than the open string. Repeat the process for the A, D, and G strings. Natural harmonics are identified with the abbreviation "Harm." between the notation and tab staves, and the notehead is a diamond instead of a circle.

Example 50

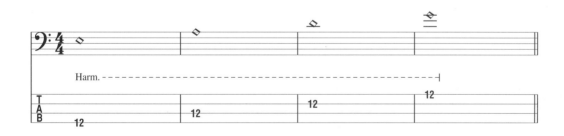

The most common application for natural harmonics is tuning the bass using harmonics at the seventh and fifth frets. To use harmonics to tune your G and D strings, pluck a harmonic at the seventh fret of the G string and the fifth fret of the D string, letting both harmonics ring together. At this location, both strings produce the pitch D. If the strings are out of tune, you'll hear the harmonics "beat" against each other in waves or pulses. The seventh fret of the D string and the fifth fret of the A string produce an A pitch, and the seventh fret of the A string and the fifth fret of the E string produce an E pitch.

Example 51

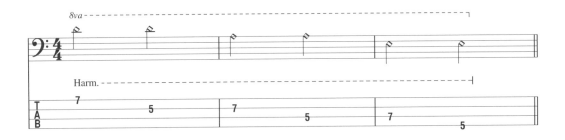

Here's a bass neck grid showing you where to find the most common harmonics up to the 12th fret. Notice that some of the harmonics are actually located in between the fret wires.

Natural Harmonic Grid

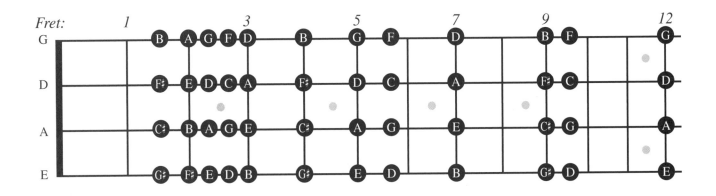

Let's play some of the natural harmonics.

Example 52

Here is a bass line incorporating natural harmonics.

Example 53

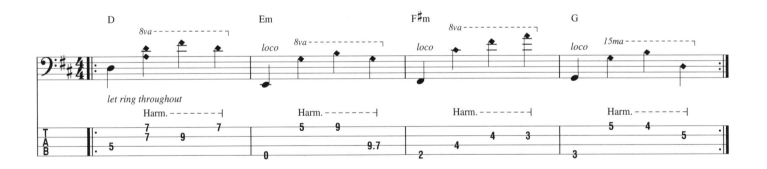

Artificial Harmonics

Artificial harmonics are played with fretted notes and require the use of your plucking hand to create the harmonic. There are two types of artificial harmonics that work well for bass: harp harmonics and tapped harmonics. Both techniques require you to fret a note with your fretting hand and then touch or tap an octave higher (12 frets) with your picking (plucking) hand. For example, if you fret at the third fret, the harmonic will be located at the 15th fret, an octave higher, or the halfway point between your fretted finger and the bridge.

Harp Harmonics

To execute a *harp harmonic*, fret a note with you fretting hand, lightly touch the harmonic point (12 frets higher) with your plucking hand's first finger, and then use another finger (or a pick) to pluck the string. When using the first finger to touch the harmonic point, for example, one can pluck the string with any available finger or use a pick that is held between your thumb and second finger. When using the thumb to touch the harmonic point, use the first finger to pluck the strings. Harp harmonics are notated with "H.H." between the notation and tab staves.

First Finger Position   Pluck Second Finger   Thumb Position

Pluck Second Finger   Pluck Thumb   Pluck Pick

Example 54

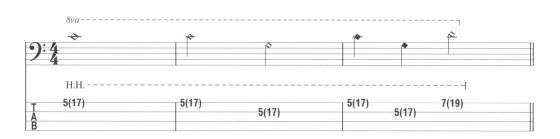

Let's work with harp harmonics in a bass line.

Example 55

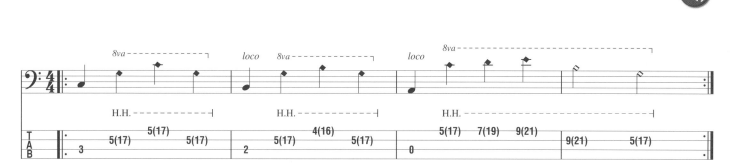

Tapped Harmonics

Tapped harmonics start the same as harp harmonics, by fretting a note, but instead of plucking the strings, you actually tap the harmonic point (12 frets higher) by quickly bouncing off the fret with a plucking-hand finger. Tap directly on the fret wire and get off as quickly as possible. Tap harmonics are notated with "A.H." between the notation and tab staves and with a "+" sign over the note in notation.

Tapped Harmonic   Tapped Harmonic Motion

Example 56

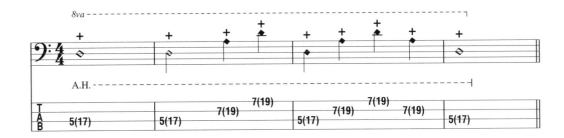

Now let's check out some tapped harmonics in a bass line.

Example 57

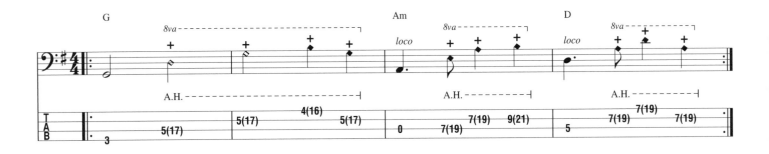

SLAP TECHNIQUES

Slap bass is an extremely popular technique for bass. It's a way for a bassist to mimic the sound of a drum kit's kick and snare. The technique has come a long way over the past several decades, so we have plenty of information to cover. There's no one absolutely correct method, and many players have slight variations on technique and approach. My best advice is to watch as many players as possible and notice how they approach and perform this technique. Try several approaches until you find what is most comfortable for you. To get you off and running, we'll be going through the basic technique of slap bass, with some generally standard advanced techniques as well.

Thumb Slap

Let's start with your thumb. Take your hand and make a loose fist. Now stick your thumb out. It should look as though you're about to hitchhike or you're giving someone the "thumbs up" sign. You'll be striking the string with the first joint of your thumb; scientifically, it's called the metacarpophalangeal joint.

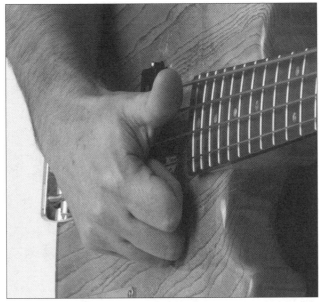

Hand Position

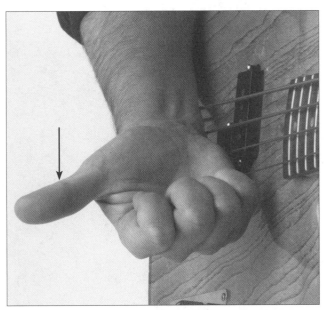

Thumb Metacarpophalangeal Joint

To execute a thumb slap, strike the string against the neck by bouncing your thumb right on the neck or just a little in front of the neck. The actual hand movement comes from your wrist/forearm—not your thumb. To give you an idea of how this works, place your "thumbs up" sign on a table, with your thumb in the air. Now hit the table with your thumb by twisting your forearm—not by bending your wrist. This is the movement you want to achieve.

There are two common ways to execute the thumb slap. We'll label them as the *bounce* and the *follow-through*. This is actually the trickiest part of slap and pop, so take your time to get it down. The first way, the bounce, involves striking the string directly in an up-down motion. The key to this movement is to strike the string and bounce off quickly so that the string rings out. The second way, the follow-through, involves striking the string in a downward motion and following through so that your thumb comes to rest on the next string. In both cases, strike the string hard enough so it gives off a percussive, clicking sound—not a plucking sound.

Bounce

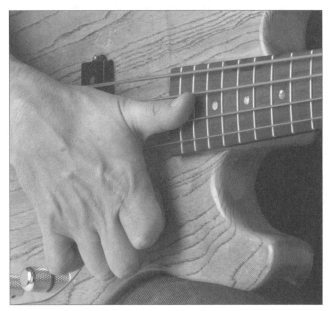

Follow-through

In this next example, I'll play it wrong initially so you can hear what it sounds like if you don't bounce or follow through quickly enough. Then I'll play it correctly. A thumb slap is notated with a "T" between the notation and tab staves.

Example 58

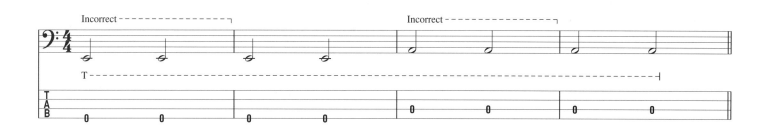

Now let's work on some thumb slaps. A great way to practice just getting the motion down is by muting the strings with your fretting hand so you can concentrate on the thumb slap in isolation.

Example 59

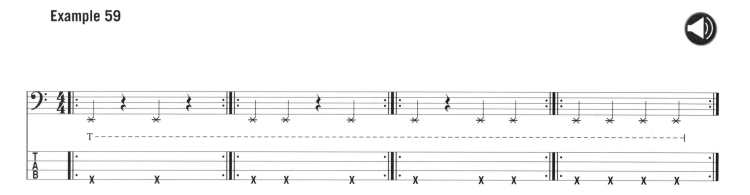

You should play the previous example on the A, D, and G strings as well. It's vitally important to execute the thumb slap on all the strings. Here are a few examples using all of the strings, with different rhythms. They will repeat at a faster tempo.

Example 60

Example 61

Example 62

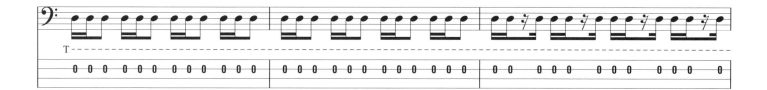

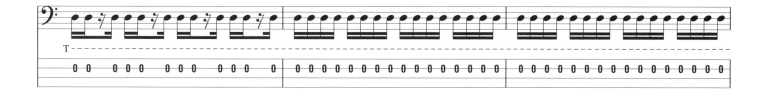

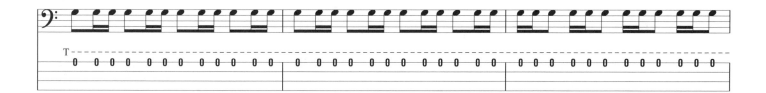

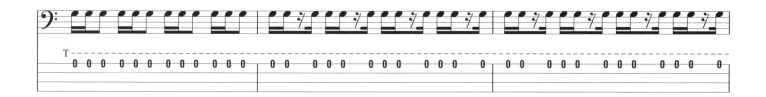

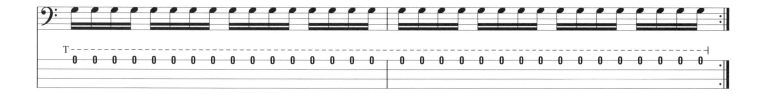

A fun way to practice this technique is to thumb slap along with songs. It's a great way to build technique and endurance while having fun!

Finger Pop

The *finger pop* technique involves snapping the string with one of your fingers to create a popping sound. You can use either your index or your middle finger to execute the finger pop. Due to the finger pop being an extension of the thumb slap, all you need to do is get your plucking hand ready. Loosen up your index or middle finger and create a hook with whichever finger you choose. Place just enough of your finger under the string to grab it and pull up. Make sure you pull just enough to get a popping sound. Popping too hard might break the string, and popping too softly will sound like a pluck instead of a pop. Hand placement for popping is located directly in front of the fingerboard, so after your extended thumb slaps the string, you can follow up with a pop in one fluid movement.

Finger Under Strings

Finger Pulling String

To get the correct motion for a finger pop, combine the thumb slap and finger pop into one motion. The movement comes from a twist or pivot of your forearm, which you've explored when thumb slapping. Mute the strings with your fret hand for this next exercise and concentrate only on the movement of your thumb and finger pop. Finger pops are notated with a "P" between notation and tab staves. This example will speed up when it repeats.

Example 63

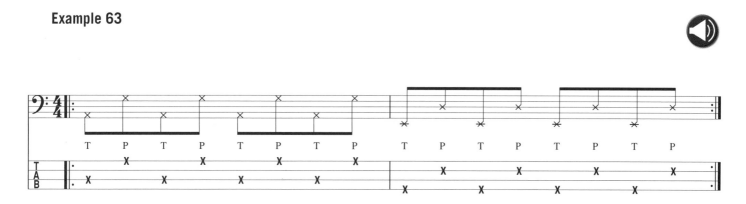

This next one is all about letting the notes ring and getting a good, solid thumb-slap and finger-pop tone.

Example 64

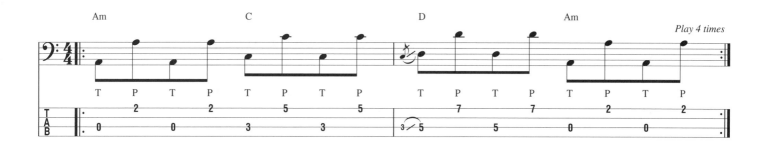

For this next example, work through each rhythm figure until you are comfortable. The entire example will repeat three times, each at a faster tempo.

Example 65

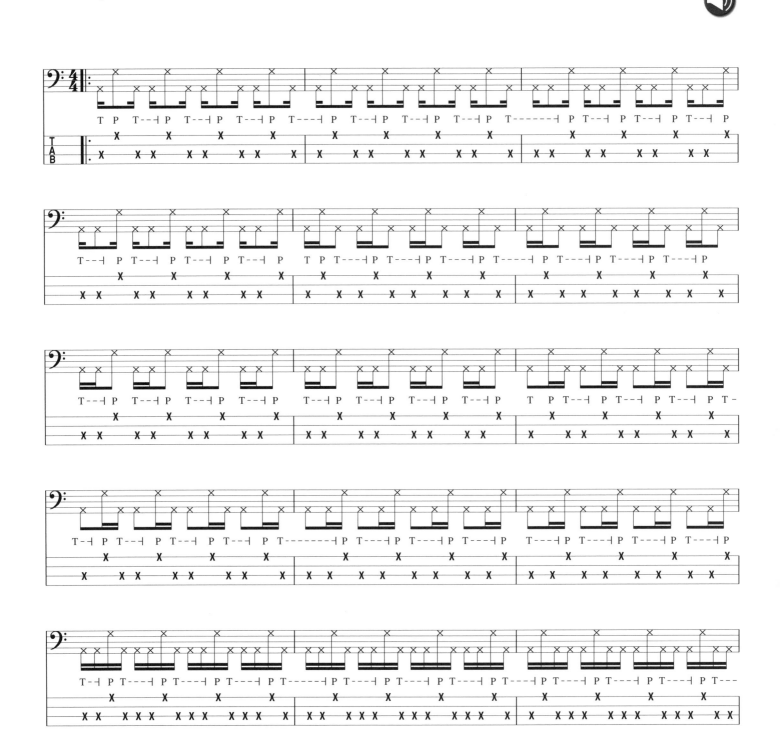

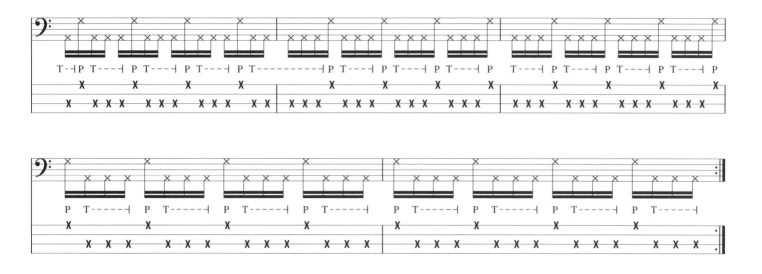

Since the previous example worked with the A and G strings, go through and work with the E and D strings as well.

Finger pops on the same string are a little trickier and most often require a slight adjustment of your popping finger and thumb to get a fluid motion. Instead of your thumb and popping finger having space between them, you have to close up your hand.

Example 66

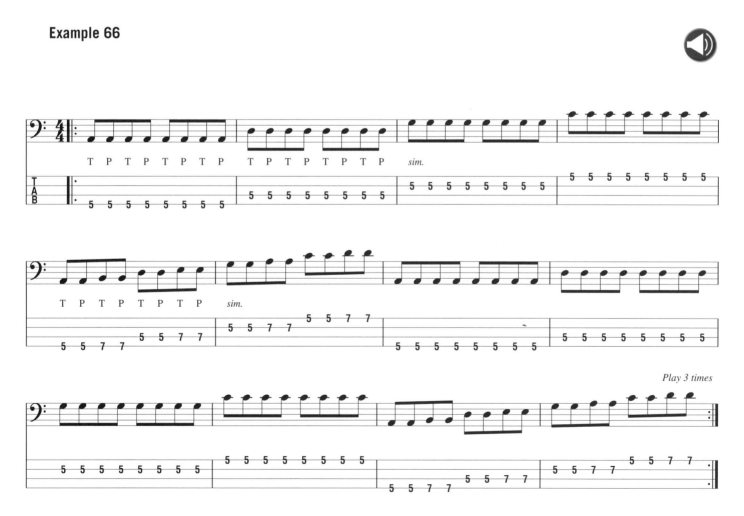

Fret-Hand Slap

The *fret-hand slap* is often referred to as the "left-hand slap". (For you lefties out there, it would be a right-hand slap, but to avoid any confusion, we'll call it the "fret-hand slap".) To perform this technique, slap your fretting hand against the fingerboard to achieve a percussive sound similar to a dead-note slap. Just like the regular slap, you want a bounce-like motion so that you don't actually fret a note. Flatten your fingers as much as possible and slap them against the fingerboard. One can come up with some pretty killer grooves using the fret-hand slap in conjunction with a normal thumb slap.

Listen to this example's audio track. I'll play a fret-hand slap the wrong way initially, followed by the correct way. Listen carefully to the difference so that, when you practice, you'll know what sound you want to develop. This can be a bit tricky and may take some time to get right. This technique is indicated by an "L" in between tab and notation.

Example 67

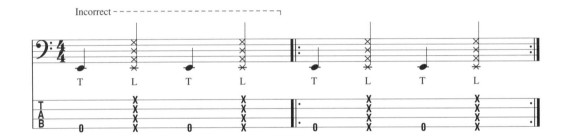

Now let's work on some common triplet patterns used with the fret-hand slap.

Example 68

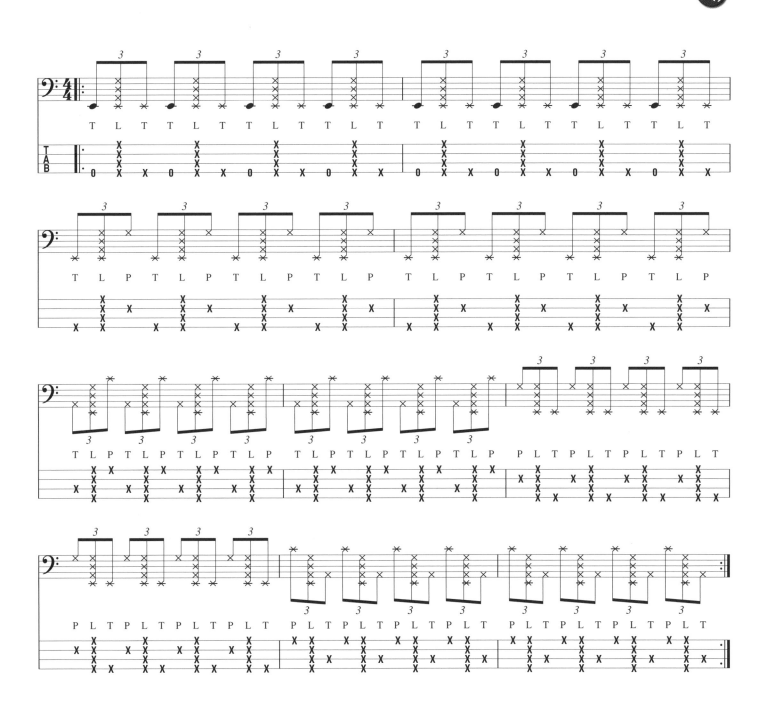

Here's the fret-hand slap in a bass line.

Example 69

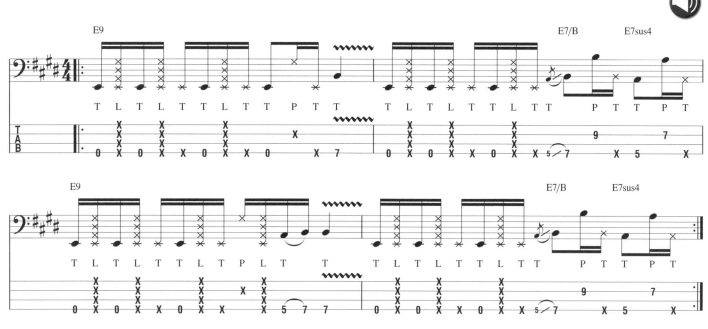

Double Thumb

For this next technique, we'll use the thumb like a pick, with a downstroke and an upstroke, but we'll do it slap-style. First, slap down with your thumb, following through until your thumb is under the string you just slapped. Then pull back up with your thumb to create a thumb pop.

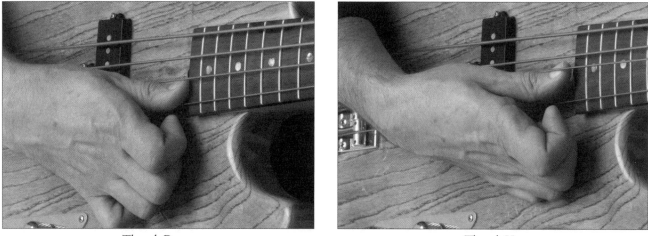

Thumb Down   Thumb Up

Now let's try a simple exercise to get started with the double-thumb technique. A thumb up-pluck is indicated by a "T↑" between notation and tab staves.

Example 70

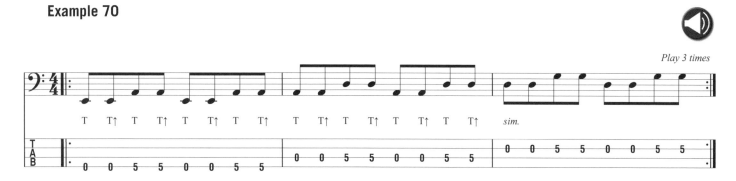

Here's a triplet using a double thumb with a finger pop. Practice this one slowly until you get into the movement of it. As you get comfortable with the movement, it will become easier and more fluid.

Example 71

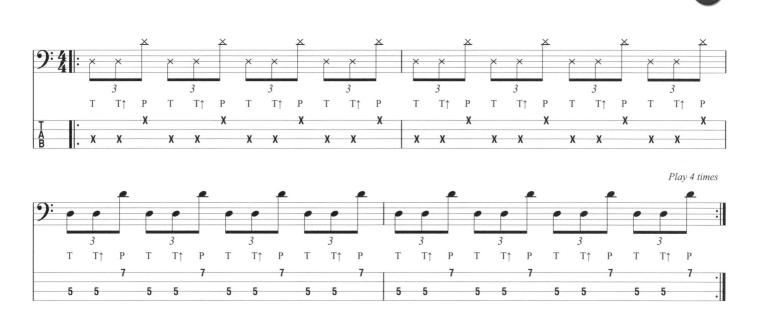

Here is a bass line using the double-thumb technique.

Example 72

Many bassists have made the double thumb a standard technique in their arsenal. It takes some time to master, but it's fun and rewarding when it becomes a natural movement.

Double Pop

The *double pop* is just that: popping the string twice, instead of once. This is accomplished by using the first and second fingers of the plucking hand. Following a thumb slap, pop with the first finger, followed by your second finger, all in one motion. Basically stated: thumb, pop, pop.

First Finger

Second Finger

Here's an exercise to get you started. Double pops are notated with "P1" (for the first finger) and "P2" (for the second finger) between the notation and tab staves. Remember to use wrist motion and make it one smooth movement. This example will increase in speed on repeats.

Example 73

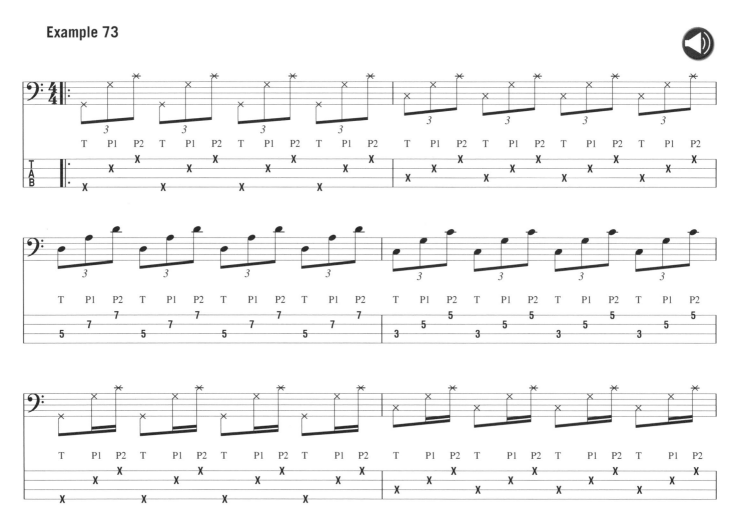

Here is a bass line incorporating double pops.

Example 74

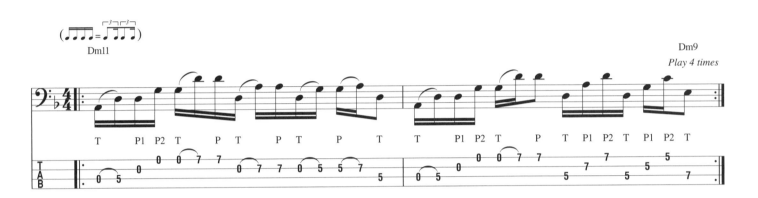

Putting It Together

Slap bass has come a long way. For proof, all one needs to do is search the web to find a multitude of various techniques and ideas. There are as many nuances as there are bassists, so remember to be open-minded and learn what others have to teach, as well as forging your own path. One of the most important ways to get any technique into your repertoire is to play grooves and experiment with different techniques. In this section, we'll put a bunch of techniques together, under the slap-bass umbrella. Learn and play the parts as written, but feel free to create your own bass lines over the grooves provided.

For this example, notice the use of staccato to make the groove short and sharp, and the use of hammer-ons and pull-offs.

Example 75

Here we use dead notes to drive a riff.

Example 76

Here's a bass line with open-string hammer-ons.

Example 77

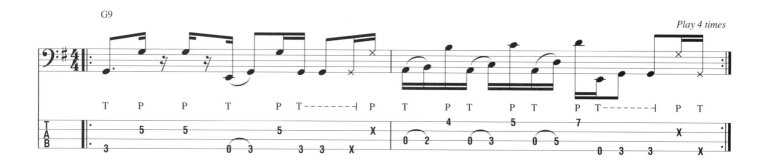

This example is a busy bass line with a plethora of slap techniques.

Example 78

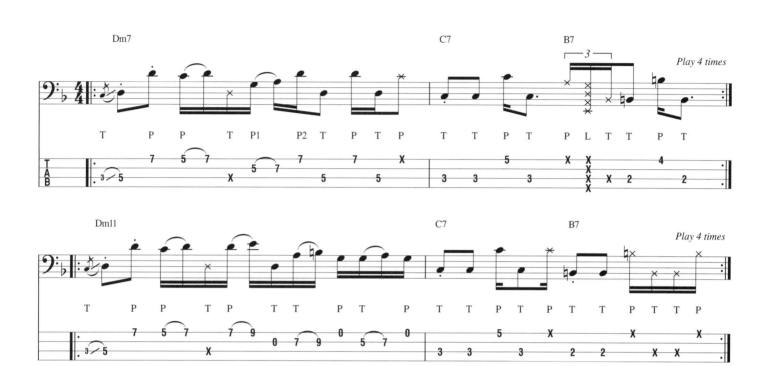

Here's a simple slap part, played over blues changes, for you to experiment with. Keeping great time and adding tasty bass fills will get you hired every time!

Example 79

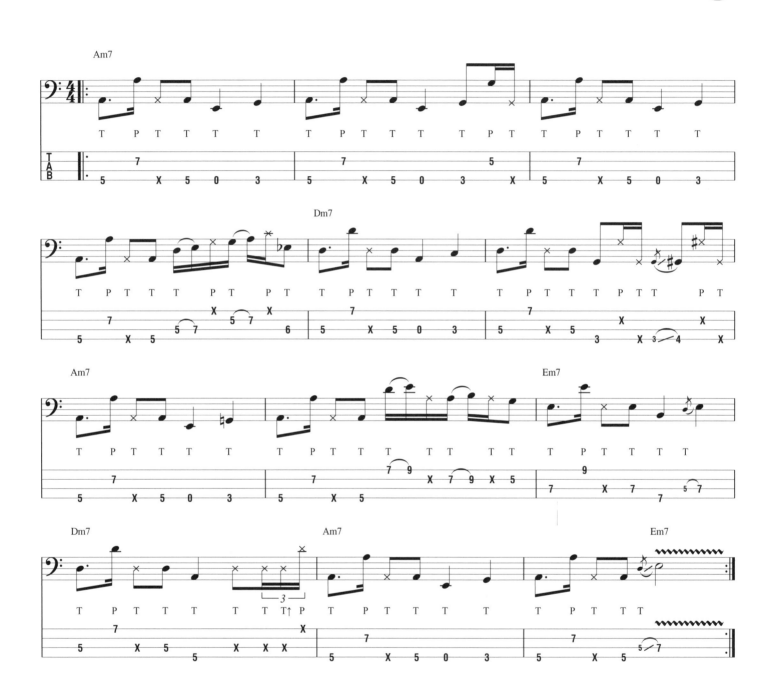

TAPPING

The *tapping* technique, like all other techniques, has been expanded into astonishing feats of awe-inspiring ability. It's a legato technique whereby fingers of the plucking hand are used to hammer on and pull off notes. There are two types of tapping: one-handed tapping and two-handed tapping.

One-Handed Tapping

One-handed tapping is performed in conjunction with the fretting hand. The plucking hand is used as an additional finger (or two) for tapping out fast passages or creating neat effects that can't be executed with the fret hand alone.

To get you started, let's look at the basic technique. Most players use their first or second finger of the plucking hand to tap. I'll refer to whichever finger you choose as simply the "tapping finger," and let you decide. Just like a hammer-on in combination with a pull-off, we'll be using your fret hand to hold a note while your tapping finger hammers on the same string and pulls off. To help with unwanted string noise, some players balance their tapping hand by anchoring their thumb on the top of the neck.

Tap

Thumb Anchor

Tapping is noted with a "+" above the note in notation and a "T" between the notation and tab staves. For the first four bars of this example, a plucking-hand tap pulls off to the first finger of the fret hand. The last three bars of this example add the third finger of the fret hand, which hammers onto the ninth fret.

Example 80

One-handed tapping is a lick-based technique usually reserved for solos or fast passages. This example features a minor triad tapping lick. It will speed up when it repeats.

Example 81

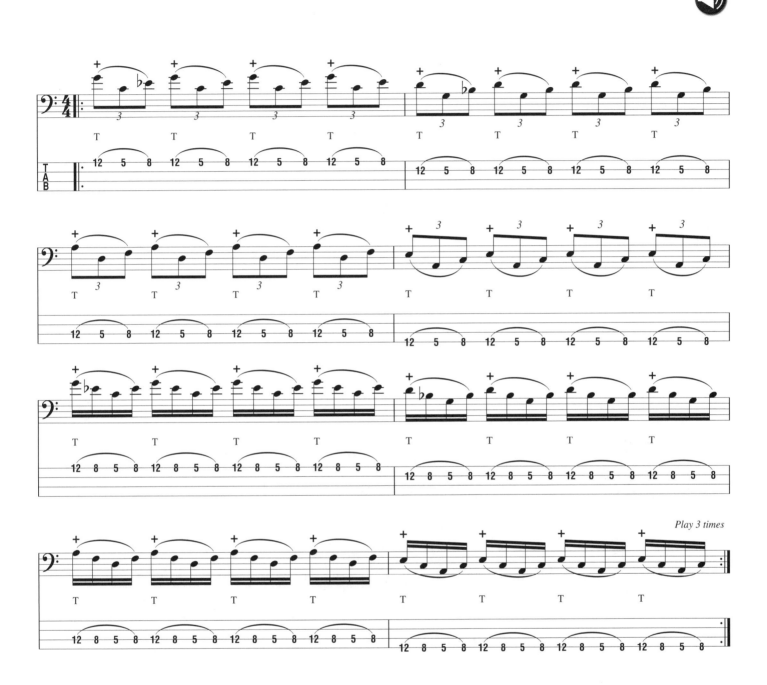

Let's work on moving up and down through the strings. This one has a hammer-on without a pluck—sometimes referred to as a "hammer-on from nowhere"—executed by the third finger of the fret hand when the lick descends.

Example 82

Play 3 times

Two-Handed Tapping

Two-handed tapping is performed when both hands tap the strings in a manner similar to the way a pianist articulates the keys of his piano, by splitting the high and low registers and being able to play counterparts. The fret hand taps the lower bass line, while the plucking hand taps out chords or melodies.

Both Hands   Plucking Hand Position (for melodies)   Plucking Hand Position (for chords)

Here's a simple, fun example using a country-style bass part with the fret hand while the plucking hand taps out the chords. The fret hand (lower register) will look normal in notation, though all notes will be hammered on, while the plucking hand will have the "+" and "T" symbols. For the tapping hand, use your first and second fingers in measures 1 and 2; when the chord changes in measures 3 and 4, use your first and third fingers. This example will repeat without bass so you can play along.

Example 83

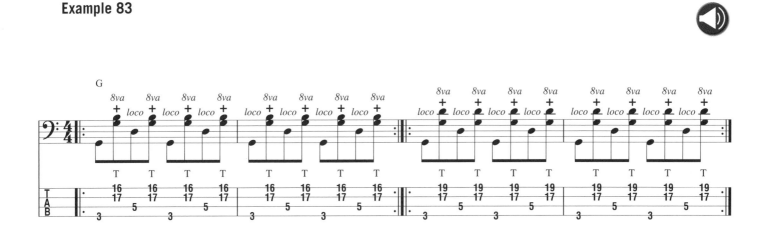

Using tapping in a supportive role can also be achieved—especially in a setting in which the chord player solos, and, as a bassist, you are left to fill the harmony.

Example 84

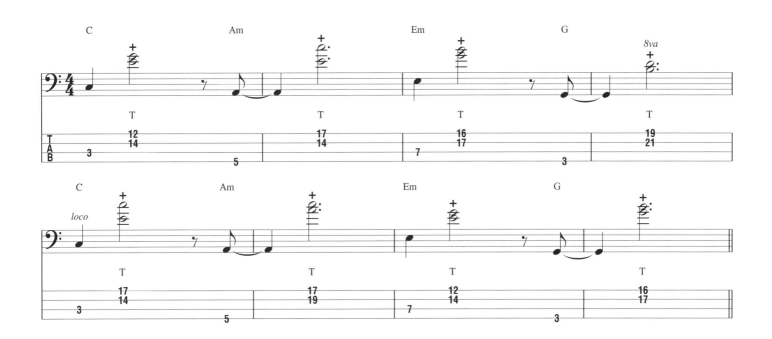

When tapping out melodies with your plucking hand, it is beneficial to work strictly on tapping out lines or scales before you start bringing in the fret hand. Here is a technical example using only the tapping/plucking hand. I suggest working out melodies, or anything else you'd like to play, with the tapping hand first, and then add the fretting hand (bass line) when you feel comfortable.

Example 85

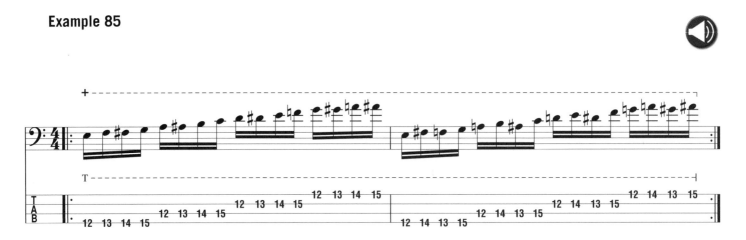

Finally, here's a bass line/melody example. The bass part is down-stemmed, and the melody is up-stemmed.

Example 86

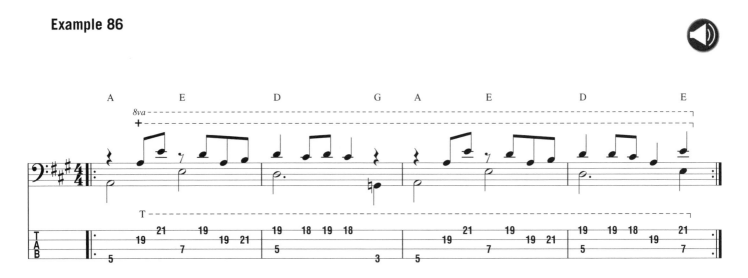

As you might imagine, the tapping technique can get pretty interesting and complicated. Multiple bassists have made careers from this technique due to the fact that they can perform solo. If it piques your curiosity, by all means, explore it further and see what you can achieve.